A WORLD OF PIZZA

Betshy Paola Sanchez

RUCKUS BOOKS

RUCKUS
B O O K S

First published in 2014
© 2014 Ruckus Books,
Thorold, ON. All rights reserved.

ISBN 978-0-9923033-6-5

Design and Production: Peter Murray
Founding Editor: Peter Murray
Author: Betshy Paola Sanchez

The author and publisher have made every effort to ensure the information contained in this book was correct at the time of going to press and accept no responsibility for any loss, injury or inconvenience sustained by any person using this book.

Images: Shutterstock & Getty Images
Recipes: www.allrecipes.com

Businesses looking to connect with their customers can work with Ruckus to develop their own custom 3D book. Cut through the noise of throw-away swag, and tired old tricks and sell your story, wrapped in your product. Or publish your catalog inside a lookalike shell and give it away. The impact is immediate, the shelf-life long, and the possibilities are endless. Contact us at ruckusbooks.com.

CONTENTS

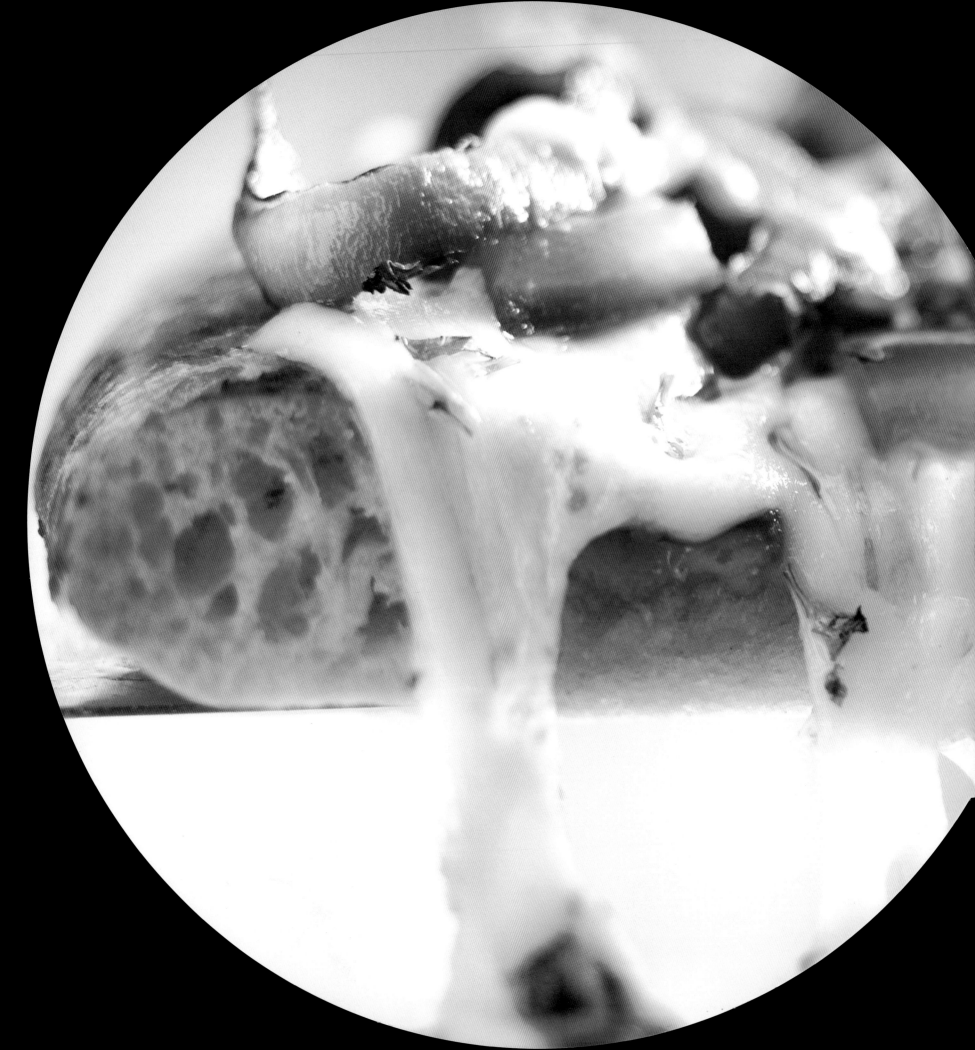

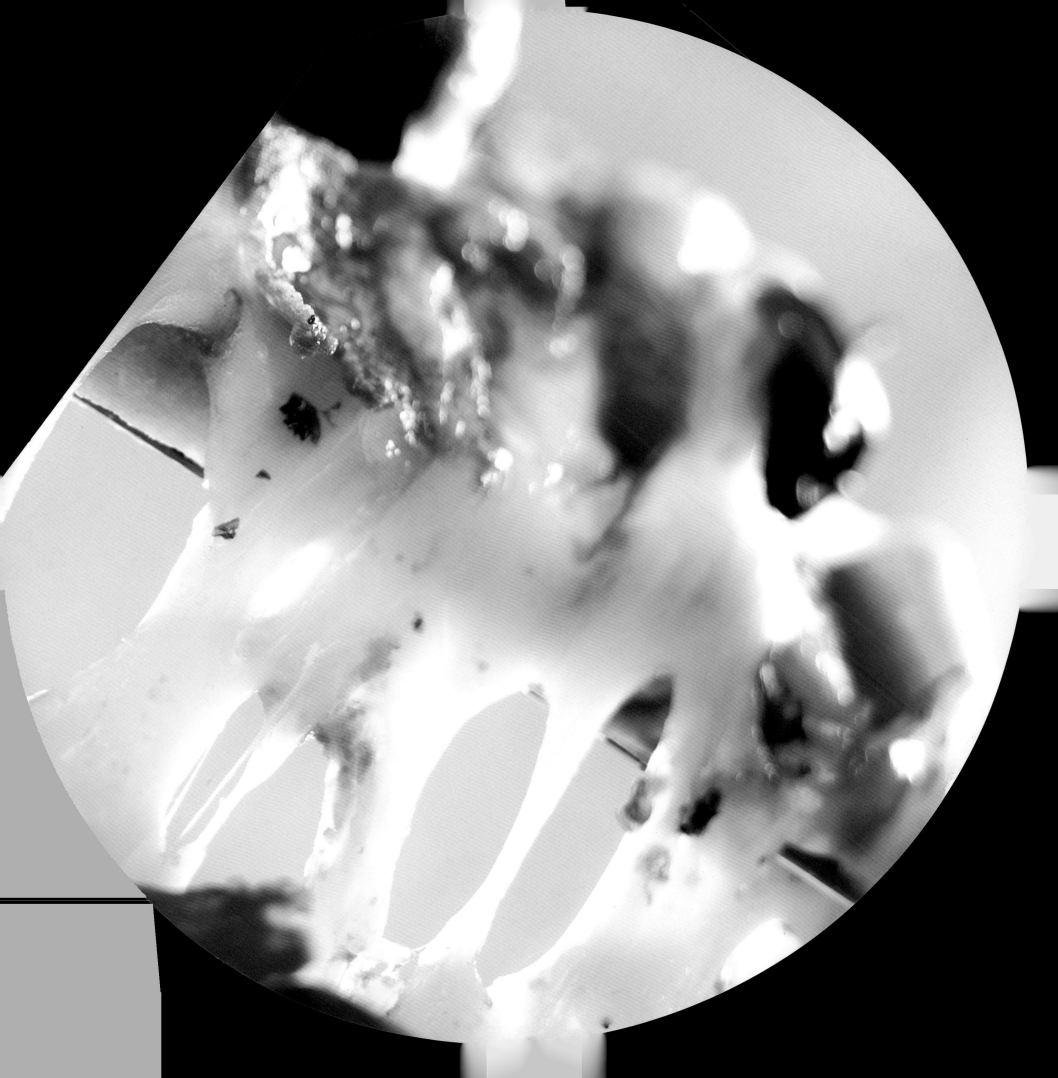

AN INTRODUCTION TO PIZZA

WHAT IS PIZZA?

A simple way to describe pizza is a food made from a layered combination of bread, tomatoes and cheese. However, this definition does not adequately illustrate the variety of ways pizza is prepared, topped and even stuffed. What was once the means of survival for a poor Neapolitan village, today is a vastly popular fast food, inexpensive and readily available.

Pizza is a multi-billion dollar industry. The phrase "let's have pizza!" is a common expression when friends, family members or colleagues gather together, ready to satisfy their hunger. It is the popular opinion that everyone loves pizza, but there are those who worry that pizza is not a healthy option. Some experts believe pizza has contributed to the current problem of obesity in the United States and other first world nations.

Have you ever wondered where pizza originated? How did it become so popular? Is pizza harmful to your health? Keep reading, and these questions will be answered.

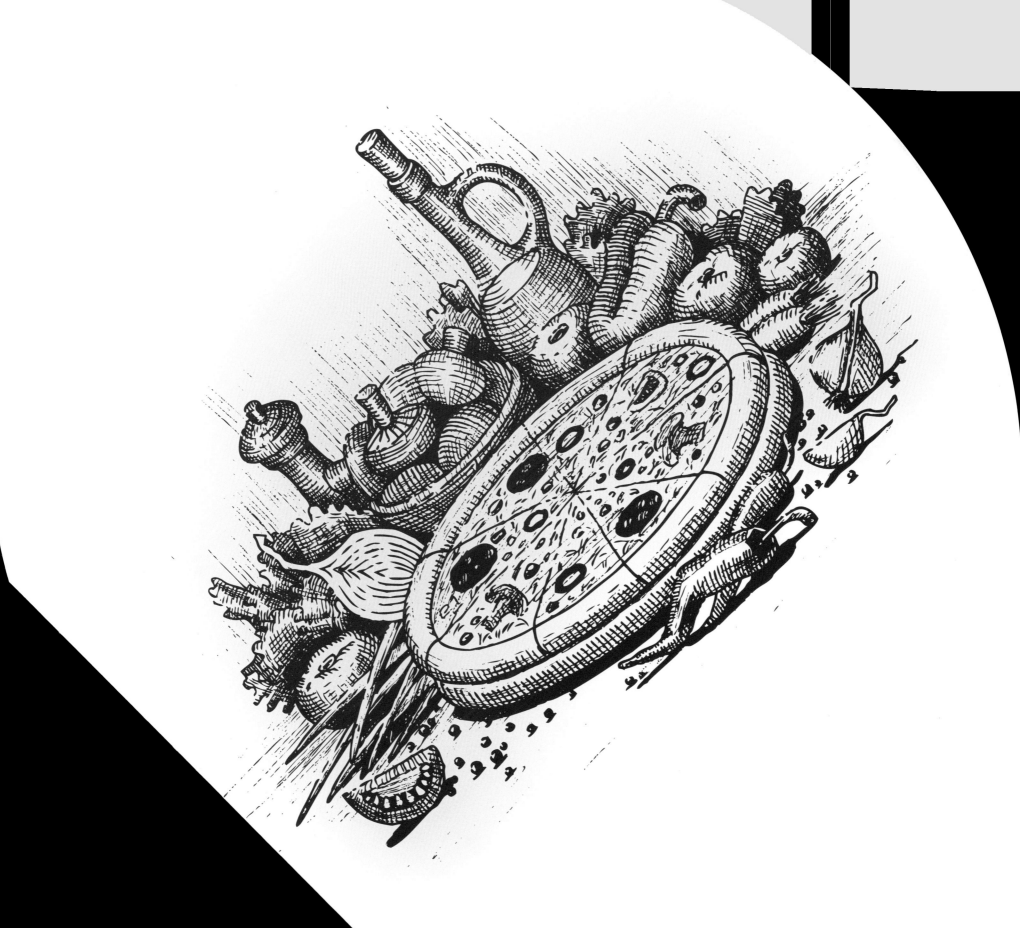

ETYMOLOGY

Much controversy surrounds the origin of the word *"pizza."* The ancient Italian word *"pizzicare"* translates into the English *"to pluck,"* and many believe this referred to the pizza being plucked out of the oven. Some scholars disagree with this explanation, arguing that the word *"pizza"* came from the ancient Greek *"pikte"* which describes fermented pastries.

A text written in 997 A.D. from Southern Italy describes the Bishop of Gaeta receiving *"duodecim pizze,"* twelve pizzas every Christmas Day and Easter Sunday from the tenants of particular properties. However, other theories include the Latin word *"pinsa"* (to crush) and *"picea"* (blackened bread from the oven), along with the Greek words *"pissa"* (to pitch) and *"ptea"* (bran bread) and the old German word *"pizzo"* (mouthful). The origin of the word *"pizza"* is decisively inconclusive.

EARLY ORIGINS OF PIZZA

If we are uncertain of where the word *"pizza"* originates, do we at least know who invented pizza? Again, this is another disputed topic. The invention of pizza is commonly attributed with the Italians, but there is evidence that suggests pizza is much older than that. Ancient Middle Eastern cultures, like the Egyptians and Babylonians, were known to consume flat, unleavened bread, baked in mud ovens. Other historians have discovered a form of pizza eaten by ancient Italian Etruscan and Mediterranean cultures. This flat bread was similar to what we call pita bread, very popular in Greece and throughout the Middle East. In his epic poem *Aeneid*, the poet Virgil speaks of *"devouring the plates on which we fed"* – believed by many to be a reference to pizza. Archeologists studying the remains of the Roman city Pompeii, which was destroyed and preserved by a volcano, stumbled upon the evidence of pizza bakeries and equipment.

However, all of these ancient pizzas were simple flatbreads with toppings. When did pizza become the dish that we consume today? Keep reading!

HISTORY & PROPAGATION OF PIZZA

In the 16th century, a form of flat bread was popular in Naples, Italy. This simple bread evolved to include various toppings as it was served in street stands, local bakeries and restaurants. When tomatoes were brought back to Europe from the newly found Americas, they became a favorite topping of the Neapolitans. The lower class would consume pizza for breakfast, lunch and dinner since it was easy to prepare and affordable, due to its simple ingredients.

Alexandre Dumas, the French travel writer and culinary expert, visited Naples and was surprised to find people not buying the entire dish of pizza. Instead, each person would only purchase the portion he could afford. Dumas believed pizza was the "gastronomic thermometer of the market," telling us much about Neapolitan society. Pizza was an integral part of the culture of poverty in Italy. People often bought it in the streets because most did not own the necessary cooking equipment. Wealthy people did not consume pizza. Famous cuisine authors of that time, such as Pellegrino Artusi, never mentioned pizza in any of their cookbooks.

The allure of pizza could not be ignored by all the aristocrats. Legend has it that Ferdinand IV of Naples (1751-1825) installed a secret oven in his palace so his wife could enjoy the unrefined food in private. However, scholars affirmed the fact that his wife, Maria Carolina, had instead banned pizzas from entering the palace. Much controversy swirled around this story, but the history of Queen Margherita sheds light on pizza's mysterious past.

It was said that Queen Margherita grew tired of the French cuisine. In 1889, she decided to visit Naples with her husband, King Umberto. The owner of a pizza restaurant, Raffaele Esposito, prepared a variety of pizzas for the royal couple. Among these choices, there was a particular pizza topped with mozzarella cheese, tomatoes and basil called "Pizza alla Mozzarella." This dish was Margherita's favourite with its colors matching the Italian flag. Eventually, this pizza was renamed "Pizza Margherita" in her honor – a variety still widely consumed today.

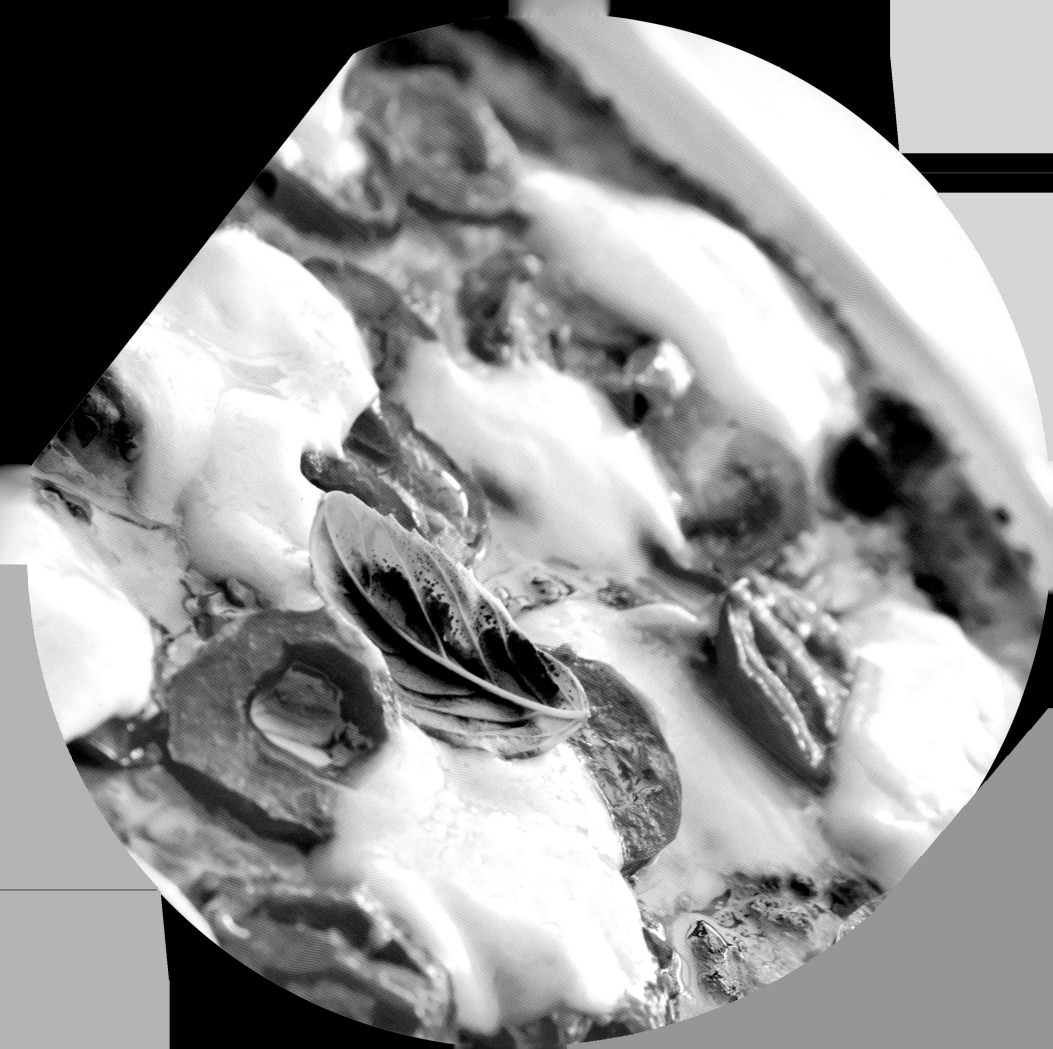

Even though embraced by royalty, the great majority of Italian people were oblivious to the taste of pizza. From the 1920s, during the Fascist era, until the end of World War II, pizza was basically ignored. In fact, in 1938, an official fascist guide to restaurants made a note about the abundance of pizza in Naples, but that it did not appear anywhere else in Italy. However, once the war was over, the consumption of pizza spread throughout the country, especially among tourists and those migrating from Naples to Northern Italy.

As pizza was spreading in popularity, the Italians still did not view it with the same relish. A few open-minded restaurant owners offered an eating tour of Italy which included the Neapolitan pizza. In 1957, an American chef, Richard Hammond, travelled through Italy and described pizza as *"those open face cheese tarts, that when the pastry is light, melt at first bite, and when it isn't seem as resistant as fibreboard"* (Helstosky, 2008). As visitors to Italy returned to their home countries, they brought with them an appetite for pizza. During the 1960s, pizza restaurants and *"make at home"* pizza kits were growing in popularity throughout Europe and even some Asian countries. But Italians as a whole were still not hungering for pizza. Famous Italian magazines and cookbooks only referred to pizza as a Neapolitan dish, if they even mentioned it at all.

Finally in the 1970s, as the Italian people started to enjoy meals outside their own homes, they discovered the delights of pizza. It was no longer a Neapolitan dish; now it was an Italian dish. Simultaneously, people from Naples were migrating to the rest of Europe, opening restaurants and serving pizza. In 1981, Italian pizza makers founded the Associazione Pizzaioli e Similari (The Association of Pizza-Makers and Such) to professionalize and ensure the quality of the pizza pie.

PIZZA CONQUERS AMERICA

From Europe, how did the humble and simple pizza migrate to America? In 1905, Gennaro Lombardi was given the license to sell this dish in New York City. However, the American people were not impressed. It was not until after World War II ended, and soldiers stationed in Italy returned home with a craving for pizza. Two entrepreneurs, Ric Riccardo and Ike Sewell, created the first "Chicago-style deep-dish pizza" in 1943. As Italian immigrants continued to move into the big cities, many made a living by holding a metal washtub filled with hot pizzas over their heads, walking up and down the streets of New York City, Chicago and Philadelphia, alluring customers with the tempting smell of the pie.

As chain restaurants were popping up all over the country, pizza was in demand. Students talked about it, children's literature mentioned it, and Hollywood food scenes included it. In fact, there were even songs written about pizza, as people crooned along with Dean Martin "when the moon hits your eye like a big pizza pie, that's amore!"

Pizza was such a craze that critiques of the time worried that it *"might replace the hot dog"* (*Helstosky, 2008*) as America's favorite fast food. Indeed, by 1970, pizza had become the nation's preferred snack food.

Founded on June 15, 1958, the first Pizza Hut was opened by brothers Frank and Dan Carney in Wichita, Kansas. By 1977, the franchise had grown to over 3000 restaurants, and international expansion was being explored. Today, it is the world's largest pizza franchise, gaining such success by diversifying their menus and recipes to accommodate the location.

People enjoyed dining out for pizza, but they also wanted the convenience of preparing pizza in their own homes, whenever the craving struck. Frozen pizza first entered the market in the 1960s, and twenty years later, there were countless varieties to suit every consumer. By 1994, pizza sales in the United States exceeded $20 billion. Everyone knew what pizza was, having tasted it and many eating it on a regular basis.

PIZZA CONQUERS THE WORLD

The creation of pizza is accredited to Italy. However, the introduction of pizza to the rest of the world is accredited to the United States. Franchises like *Pizza Hut* and *Domino's Pizza* expanded internationally. They preached the concept of standardized pizza – a large pizza meant to be shared with family and friends, and cut into slices to be eaten by hand.

However, as pizza crossed geographical borders, it became less and less standardized. Global consumers redefined pizza according to their own cultural tastes, although these changes were often carried out by corporate executives. The propagation of pizza around the world was all about technology, creativity and ultimately, profit. As pizza consumption rose, the recipes were adapted to the unique cultural and economic features of each country. The original pizza recipes would go through the experimentation process as consumers voiced their preferences. However, one pizza recipe did not change. The original Margherita pizza, with its simple toppings of cheese, basil and tomatoes, remained unmodified, except for the variation from mozzarella to other cheeses.

Pizza's popularity continued to expand. It was first introduced to Japan in the 1970s. The Japanese welcomed this new dish, giving it their own twist on the toppings: squid, corn, potatoes, mayonnaise and even rice balls. From Japan, pizza franchises were spreading to China, the Soviet Union and Pakistan. In 2001, the first pizza was even delivered to Russian astronauts aboard the International Space Station, a $1 million promotional stunt by *Pizza Hut*. Islamic countries also enjoyed the taste of pizza, but because of religious restrictions, the pork toppings were forbidden, including ham, pepperoni and salami.

Over time, the quality of pizza became increasingly irrelevant. People all over the globe started to eat more and more pizza because it was inexpensive, expedient to prepare and filled empty stomachs. It can be said that pizza changed the way the world saw food.

PIZZA TODAY

Today, America is among the world's top consumers of pizza, eating the equivalent of one hundred acres each day. The U.S. Department of Agriculture states that one in eight Americans consume pizza on any given day, the number rising to more than one in four males, ages 6-19. According to the 2010 and 2013 Restaurant, Food & Beverage Market Research Handbooks, "*the pizza industry is a $40 billion-a-year business*" with more than three billion pizza pies sold every year in the United States. The three leading worldwide franchises are Pizza Hut ($10.4 billion annual revenue, 13,175 branches), Domino's Pizza ($5.5 billion annual revenue, 8,773 branches) and Papa John's Pizza ($2.3 annual revenue, 3,380 branches). Due to the American influence, more people worldwide have tried pepperoni pizza than Italy's original Neapolitan pizza.

Throughout 2008 and 2009, significant losses were recorded in the pizza industry, leading some experts to believe it was in decline. However, price promotions helped to recover some of those losses in 2010. Today, there is a notable increase in pizza sales. Technological advances, like online ordering and mobile phones, have simplified and facilitated pizza delivery, increasing sales. In total, the pizza industry represents 11.7% of all restaurants and more than 10% of all food services sales.

Effective marketing of pizza brands is crucial in this competitive industry, as promotions are created and delivered through direct mail, magazines, newspapers, print coupons, TV commercials, etc. The pizza industry is one of the first to use social media to gain and maintain customers. The increase in Internet use has made it necessary for companies to set up a significant presence on the web. Social networking sites, such as Facebook and Twitter, play a major role in the promotion and advertising of a particular pizza restaurant. For many people, their first morning activity is checking their social news feeds, "liking" and "re-tweeting" those they find interesting, giving this online "word of mouth" powerful influence.

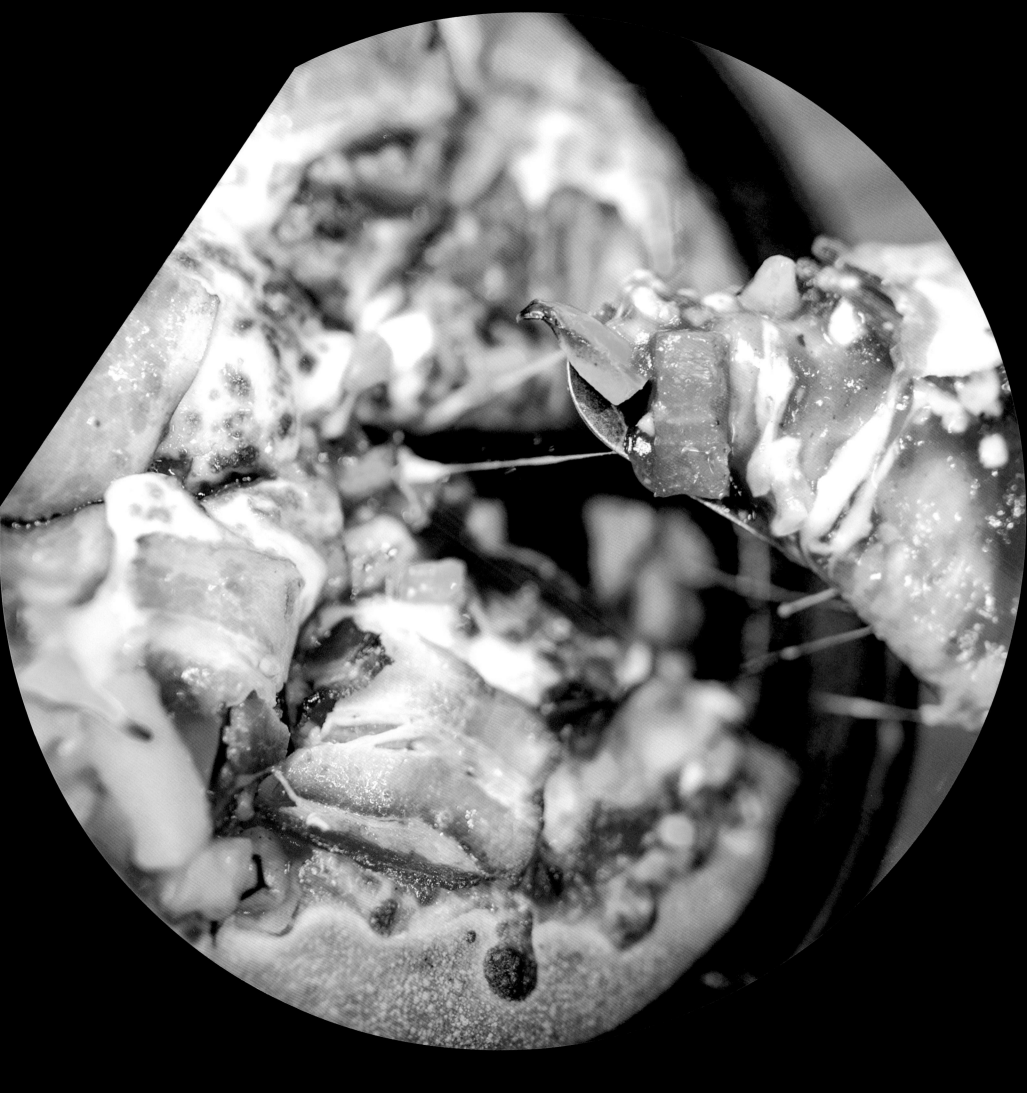

Social media marketing of pizza companies encourages people to share promotional news with family and friends, hoping to create an Internet viral effect of a restaurant's price deals or fresh menu items.

People often look for recommendations about specific restaurants before visiting a new establishment. To maintain their reputation, pizza restaurants are careful to promote confidence through solid recommendations. There is a positive correlation between a restaurant's social media reviews and its earnings. Too many poor reviews can mean the end of a pizzeria. Leading pizza brands have even assigned employees with the specific task of engaging customers, promoting the restaurant and building a loyal online audience. Successful pizza restaurants need to continue utilizing the ever-changing mode of social media to amplify their image.

THE PREPARATION OF PIZZA

HOW IS PIZZA MADE?

One of the best loved foods in the world, pizza is offered in many forms: whole pies, by the slice or frozen. What makes this dish so special? What are the basic ingredients? What is its health value? Let's find out.

THE BASIC INGREDIENTS OF PIZZA

At its most basic level, pizza is cheese, bread and tomatoes, the main ingredients of the Margherita pizza. The first ingredient, cheese, has countless varieties, but it is believed that the buffalo mozzarella was the original Naples choice. Mozzarella has a mild flavor to complement a variety of toppings and a smooth consistency, that when melted allows it to stretch. Creative recipes substitute pecorino, romano, ricotta and scamorza cheeses, even combining two or more together, giving the pizza a gourmet flavor. In different cultures, the local cheese is often utilized, so the pizza will have a unique taste for each region.

The second key ingredient of the basic pizza is bread. Making the perfect pizza crust has become an art for many chefs, mixing the flour, water, salt and yeast precisely and allowing the dough necessary time to rise. By adding a small amount of olive oil or shortening, a chef can increase the thickness of the crust (for example, a Neapolitan thin crust has no oil at all). A high level of gluten in the flour gives the dough its characteristic stretchy consistency. Kneading the dough allows the gluten protein to bind the dough together, given it strength and cohesion. For many, the time and energy necessary to make their own pizza dough is not practical, and they opt for the readily available frozen pizza dough from their local grocer.

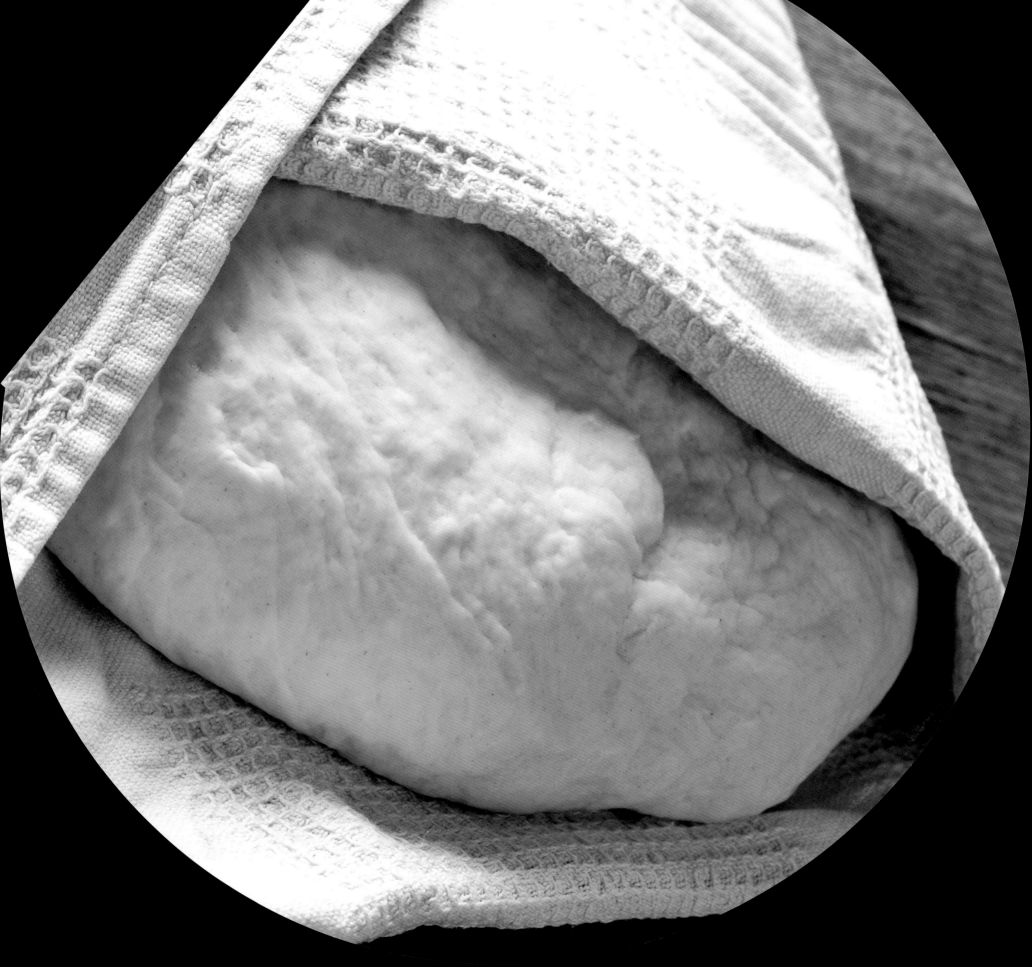

Tomatoes are the final ingredient necessary to create a basic pizza pie. Italians have been using tomatoes since the 18th century, typically crushing them for the topping. Today, pizza is usually covered not with whole tomatoes, but a cooked tomato sauce seasoned with herbs and spices. Pizza sauces allow chefs to expand their imaginations as they experiment with garlic, basil, oregano and olive oil. Making your own sauce at home allows you to eliminate the additives or preservatives found in store-bought varieties.

There are many different techniques used to prepare the pizza. Centuries ago, pizza was baked in a primitive brick oven. Today, you can bake your pizza at home in a conventional oven, using cookie sheets or ideally ceramic stoneware. Grilling pizza on the barbeque has become popular because the results are similar to a wood fired oven. Those who are really serious about their pizza can invest in an indoor or outdoor pizza oven to create pizzeria-quality pies.

HEALTH CONSIDERATIONS

The war on obesity is being waged in the United States and other first world countries. While there are numerous factors attributing to the rise of obesity, researchers do link this increase to our convenience food, including pizza. Experts base their concerns on the high levels of calories, fat and salt, especially found in mass-produced pizzas. According to the U.S. Department of Agriculture's National Nutrient Database, a slice of restaurant cheese pizza, weighing 103 g, contains 272 calories with 9.8 g of fat and 551 mg of sodium, and that does not include any extra toppings.

However, pizza can actually be a nutritious meal choice. Preparing your pizza at home can eliminate many of the empty calories, allowing for a more healthy option. Using whole wheat flour in the crust will provide you with a good source of fibre. Just be careful that you use a virgin olive oil, avoiding the hydrogenated oils. In fact, tomato sauce is packed with vitamin C and antioxidants. Fresh studies show that lycopene, a vital antioxidant which fights potential cancer-causing free radicals, is better absorbed by the body when tomatoes are cooked. Cheese is an excellent source of calcium and protein, but sprinkle conservatively as it is also high in fat. Topping your pizza with vegetables like peppers, onions, broccoli or zucchini will add an extra dose of vitamins and minerals. Add some meat too; only be sure to use meat that is low in saturated fat and sodium. Overall, when dining on pizza, the key is moderation: limit yourself to one or two moderate size slices.

Although vilified by some, pizza has not lost its place in our hearts as the ultimate comfort food. Just the aroma of fresh pizza can cause our mouths to water. By using the recipes provided, you will discover the delights of making your own pizza. Do not be afraid to experiment with different sauces, toppings and cheeses as you concoct your own unique creations.

LET YOUR TASTE BUDS BE YOUR GUIDE AS YOU EXPLORE THE WORLD OF PIZZA!

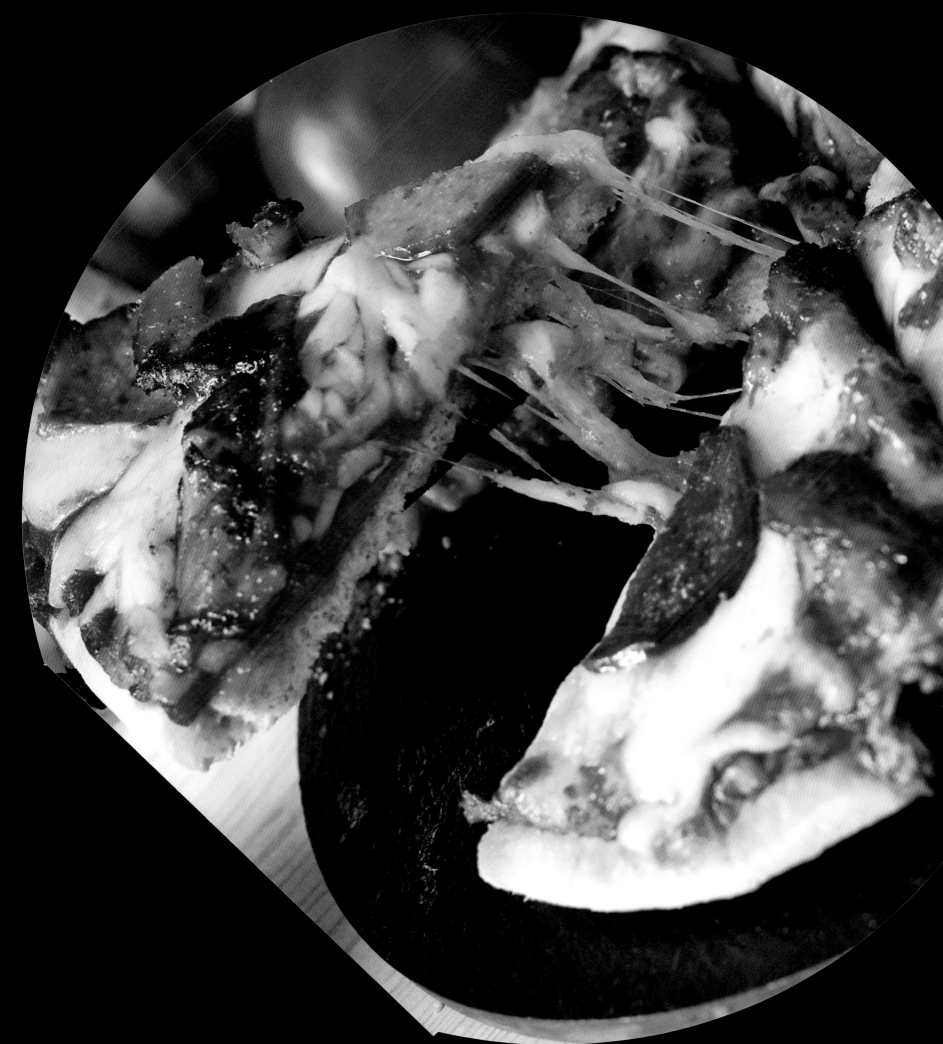

DELICIOUS RECIPES

GARDEN VEGGIE PIZZA SQUARES

Original recipe makes 48 squares

INGREDIENTS

» 1 (8 ounce) package refrigerated crescent rolls
» 1 (8 ounce) package cream cheese, softened
» 1 (1 ounce) package Ranch-style dressing mix

» 2 carrots, finely chopped
» 1/2 cup chopped red bell peppers
» 1/2 cup chopped green bell pepper
» 1/2 cup fresh broccoli, chopped
» 1/2 cup chopped green onions

DIRECTIONS

1. Preheat oven to 375 degrees F (190 degrees C). Roll out crescent rolls onto a large non-stick baking sheet. Stretch and flatten to form a single rectangular shape on the baking sheet. Bake 11 to 13 minutes in the preheated oven, or until golden brown. Allow to cool.

2. Place cream cheese in a medium bowl. Mix cream cheese with 1/2 of the ranch dressing mix. Adjust the amount of dressing mix to taste. Spread the mixture over the cooled crust. Arrange carrots, red bell pepper, broccoli and green onions on top. Chill in the refrigerator approximately 1 hour. Cut into bite-size squares to serve.

Source: Allrecipes.com

FOUR CHEESE MARGHERITA PIZZA

Original recipe makes two pizzas

INGREDIENTS

» 1/4 cup olive oil
» 1 tablespoon minced garlic
» 1/2 teaspoon sea salt
» 8 Roma tomatoes, sliced
» 2 (12 inch) pre-baked pizza crusts
» 8 ounces shredded Mozzarella cheese
» 4 ounces shredded Fontina cheese
» 10 fresh basil leaves, washed, dried
» 1/2 cup freshly grated Parmesan cheese
» 1/2 cup crumbled feta cheese

DIRECTIONS

1. Stir together olive oil, garlic, and salt; toss with tomatoes, and allow to stand for 15 minutes. Preheat oven to 400 degrees F (200 degrees C).

2. Brush each pizza crust with some of the tomato marinade. Sprinkle the pizzas evenly with Mozzarella and Fontina cheeses. Arrange tomatoes overtop, then sprinkle with shredded basil, Parmesan, and feta cheese.

3. Bake in preheated oven until the cheese is bubbly and golden brown, about 10 minutes.

JIMMY'S MEXICAN PIZZA

Original recipe makes eight servings

INGREDIENTS

- 1/2 pound ground beef
- 1 medium onion, diced
- 1 clove garlic, minced
- 1 tablespoon chili powder
- 1 teaspoon ground cumin
- 1 teaspoon paprika
- 1/2 teaspoon black pepper
- 1/2 teaspoon salt
- 1 (16 ounce) can refried beans
- 4 (10 inch) flour tortillas

- 1/2 cup salsa
- 1 cup shredded Cheddar cheese
- 1 cup shredded Monterey Jack cheese
- 2 green onions, chopped
- 2 roma (plum) tomatoes, diced
- 1/4 cup thinly sliced jalapeno pepper
- 1/4 cup sour cream (optional)

Directions displayed on next page

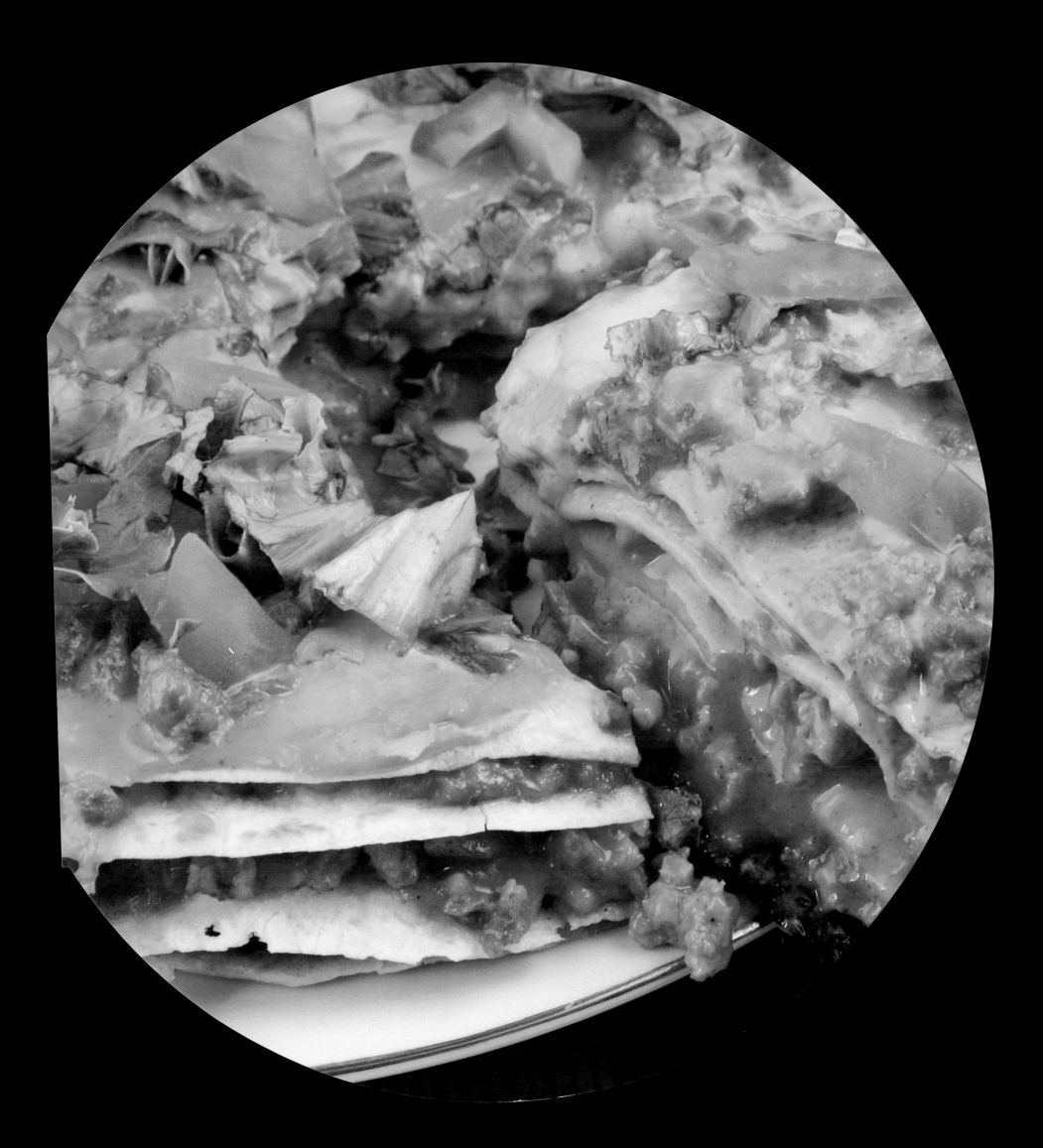

JIMMY'S MEXICAN PIZZA

Continued from previous page

DIRECTIONS

1. Preheat the oven to 350 degrees F (175 degrees C). Coat 2 pie plates with non-stick cooking spray.

2. Place beef, onion and garlic in a skillet over medium heat. Cook until beef is evenly browned. Drain off grease. Season the meat with chili powder, cumin, paprika, salt and pepper.

3. Lay one tortilla in each pie plate, and cover with a layer of refried beans. Spread half of the seasoned ground beef over each one, and then cover with a second tortilla. Bake for 10 minutes in the preheated oven. Remove the plates from the oven, and let cool slightly. Spread half of the salsa over each top tortilla. Cover each pizza with half of the Cheddar and Monterey Jack cheeses. Place half of the tomatoes, half of the green onions, and half of the jalapeno slices onto each one.

4. Return the pizzas to the oven, and bake for 5 to 10 more minutes, until the cheese is melted. Remove from the oven, and let cool slightly before slicing each one into 4 pieces.

Source: Allrecipes.com

FRUIT PIZZA

Original recipe makes one fruit pizza

INGREDIENTS

- 1/2 cup butter, softened
- 3/4 cup white sugar
- 1 egg
- 1 1/4 cups all-purpose flour
- 1 teaspoon cream of tartar
- 1/2 teaspoon baking soda
- 1/4 teaspoon salt
- 1 (8 ounce) package cream cheese
- 1/2 cup white sugar
- 2 teaspoons vanilla extract

DIRECTIONS

1. Preheat oven to 350 degrees F (175 degrees C).
2. In a large bowl, cream together the butter and 3/4 cup sugar until smooth. Mix in egg. combine the flour, cream of tartar, baking soda and salt; stir into the creamed mixture until just blended. Press dough into an ungreased pizza pan.
3. Bake in preheated oven for 8 to 10 minutes, or until lightly browned. Cool.
4. In a large bowl, beat cream cheese with 1/2 cup sugar and vanilla until light. Spread on cooled crust.
5. Arrange desired fruit on top of filling, and chill.

Source: Allrecipes.com

VEGGIE PIZZA

Original recipe makes one pizza

INGREDIENTS

» 2 (8 ounce) packages refrigerated crescent rolls
» 2 (8 ounce) packages cream cheese, softened
» 1 cup mayonnaise
» 1 (1 ounce) package dry Ranch-style dressing mix
» 1 cup fresh broccoli, chopped
» 1 cup chopped tomatoes
» 1 cup chopped green bell pepper
» 1 cup chopped cauliflower
» 1 cup shredded carrots
» 1 cup shredded Cheddar cheese

DIRECTIONS

1. Preheat oven to 375 degrees F (190 degrees C).
2. Roll out the crescent roll dough onto a 9x13 inch baking sheet, and pinch together edges to form the pizza crust. Bake crust for 12 minutes in the preheated oven. Once finished cooking, remove crust from oven and let cool 15 minutes without removing it from the baking sheet.
3. In a small mixing bowl, combine cream cheese, mayonnaise, and dry Ranch dressing. Spread the mixture over the cooled crust. Arrange broccoli, tomato, green bell pepper, cauliflower, shredded carrots, and Cheddar cheese over the cream cheese layer. Chill for one hour, slice and serve.

Source: Allrecipes.com

PITA PIZZA

Original recipe makes one pizza

INGREDIENTS

» 1 pita bread round
» 1 teaspoon olive oil
» 3 tablespoons pizza sauce
» 1/4 cup sliced crimini mushrooms
» 1/2 cup shredded mozzarella cheese
» 1/8 teaspoon garlic salt

DIRECTIONS

1. Preheat grill for medium-high heat.
2. Spread one side of the pita with olive oil and pizza sauce. Top with cheese and mushrooms, and season with garlic salt.
3. Lightly oil grill grate. Place pita pizza on grill, cover, and cook until cheese completely melts, about 5 minutes.

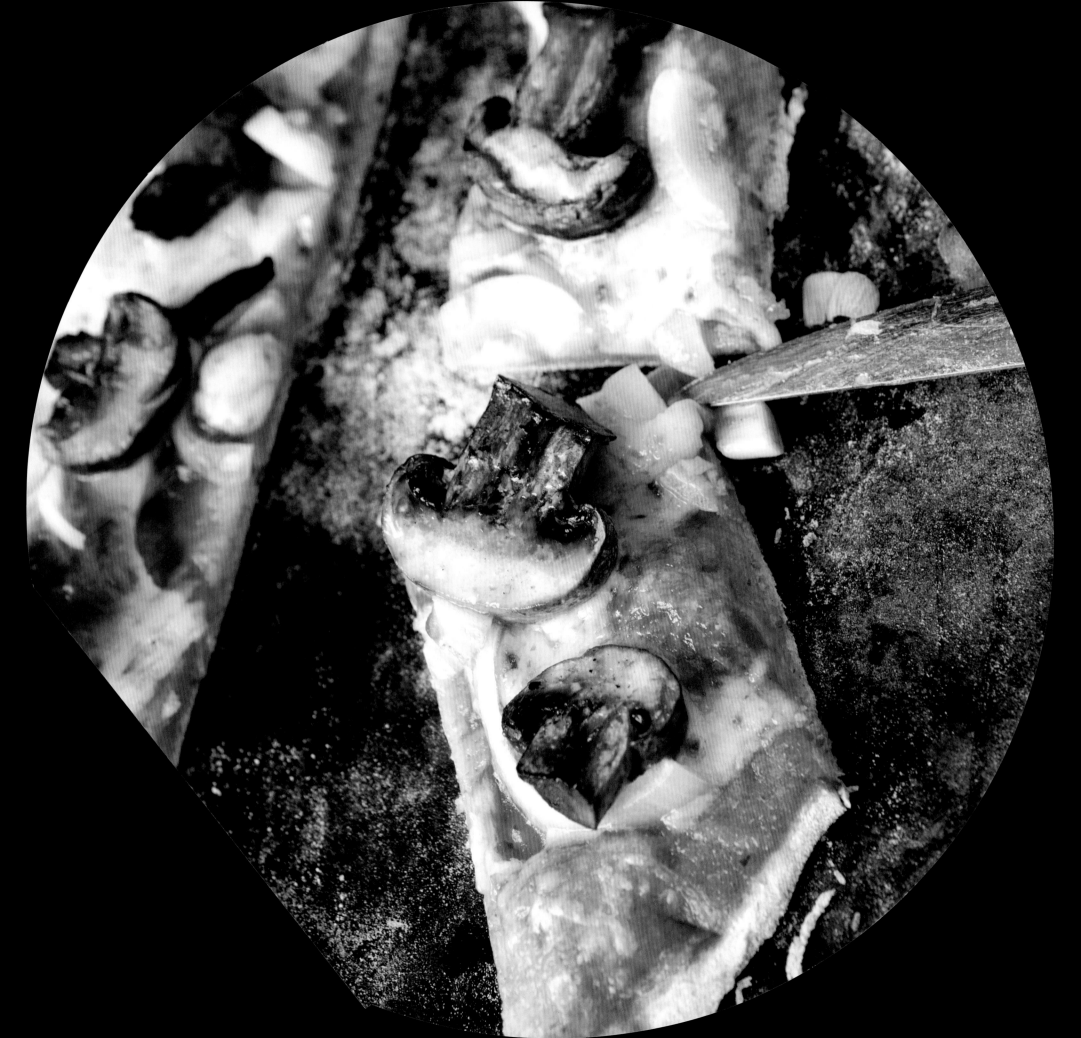

GOURMET CHICKEN PIZZA

Original recipe makes one pizza

INGREDIENTS

» 2 skinless, boneless chicken breast halves
» 1 (10 ounce) can refrigerated pizza crust
» 1/2 cup Ranch-style salad dressing
» 1 cup shredded mozzarella cheese
» 1 cup shredded Cheddar cheese
» 1 cup chopped tomatoes
» 1/4 cup chopped green onions

DIRECTIONS

1. Preheat oven to 425 degrees F (220 degrees C). Lightly grease a pizza pan or medium baking sheet.

2. Place chicken in a large skillet over medium-high heat. Cook until no longer pink, and juices run clear. Cool, then either shred or chop into small pieces.

3. Unroll dough, and press into the prepared pizza pan or baking sheet. Bake crust for 7 minutes in the preheated oven, or until it begins to turn golden brown. Remove from oven. Spread ranch dressing over partially baked crust. Sprinkle on mozzarella cheese. Place tomatoes, green onion, and chicken on top of mozzarella cheese, then top with Cheddar cheese. Return to the oven for 20 to 25 minutes, until cheese is melted and bubbly.

Source: Allrecipes.com

PESTO PIZZA

Original recipe makes six servings

INGREDIENTS

- 1 (12 inch) pre-baked pizza crust
- 1/2 cup pesto
- 1 ripe tomato, chopped
- 1/2 cup green bell pepper, chopped
- 1/2 small red onion, chopped
- 1 (2 ounce) can chopped black olives, drained
- 1 (4 ounce) can artichoke hearts, drained and sliced
- 1 cup crumbled feta cheese

DIRECTIONS

1. Preheat oven to 450 degrees F (230 degrees C).
2. Spread pesto on pizza crust. Top with tomatoes, bell peppers, olives, red onions, artichoke hearts and feta cheese.
3. Bake for 8 to 10 minutes, or until cheese is melted and browned.

BUFFALO STYLE CHICKEN PIZZA

Original recipe makes six servings

INGREDIENTS

» 3 skinless, boneless chicken breast halves - cooked and cubed
» 2 tablespoons butter, melted
» 1 (8 ounce) bottle blue cheese salad dressing
» 1 (2 ounce) bottle hot sauce
» 1 (16 inch) prepared pizza crust
» 1 (8 ounce) package shredded mozzarella cheese

DIRECTIONS

1. Preheat oven to 425 degrees F (220 degrees C).
2. In a medium bowl combine the cubed chicken, melted butter and hot sauce. Mix well. Spread whole bottle of salad dressing over crust, then top with chicken mixture and sprinkle with shredded cheese.
3. Bake in preheated oven until crust is golden brown and cheese is bubbly, about 5 to 10 minutes. Let set a few minutes before slicing, and serve.

Source: Allrecipes.com

PIZZA ON THE GRILL

Original recipe makes 16 servings

INGREDIENTS

- » 1 (.25 ounce) package active dry yeast
- » 1 cup warm water
- » 1 pinch white sugar
- » 2 teaspoons kosher salt
- » 1 tablespoon olive oil
- » 3 1/3 cups all-purpose flour
- » 2 cloves garlic, minced
- » 1 tablespoon chopped fresh basil

- » 1/2 cup olive oil
- » 1 teaspoon minced garlic
- » 1/4 cup tomato sauce
- » 1 cup chopped tomatoes
- » 1/4 cup sliced black olives
- » 1/4 cup roasted red peppers
- » 2 cups shredded mozzarella cheese
- » 4 tablespoons chopped fresh basil

Directions displayed on next page

Source: Allrecipes.com

PIZZA ON THE GRILL

Continued from previous page

DIRECTIONS

1. In a bowl, dissolve yeast in warm water, and mix in sugar. Proof for ten minutes, or until frothy. Mix in the salt, olive oil, and flour until dough pulls away from the sides of the bowl. Turn onto a lightly floured surface. Knead until smooth, about 8 minutes. Place dough in a well oiled bowl, and cover with a damp cloth. Set aside to rise until doubled, about 1 hour. Punch down, and knead in garlic and basil. Set aside to rise for 1 more hour, or until doubled again.

2. Preheat grill for high heat. Heat olive oil with garlic for 30 seconds in the microwave. Set aside. Punch down dough, and divide in half. Form each half into an oblong shape 3/8 to 1/2 inch thick. Brush grill grate with garlic flavored olive oil. Carefully place one piece of dough on hot grill. The dough will begin to puff almost immediately. When the bottom crust has lightly browned, turn the dough over using two spatulas. Working quickly, brush oil over crust, and then brush with 2 tablespoons tomato sauce. Arrange 1/2 cup chopped tomatoes, 1/8 cup sliced black olives, and 1/8 cup roasted red peppers over crust. Sprinkle with 1 cup cheese and 2 tablespoons basil. Close the lid, and cook until the cheese melts. Remove from grill, and set aside to cool for a few minutes while you prepare the second pizza.

Source: Allrecipes.com

74

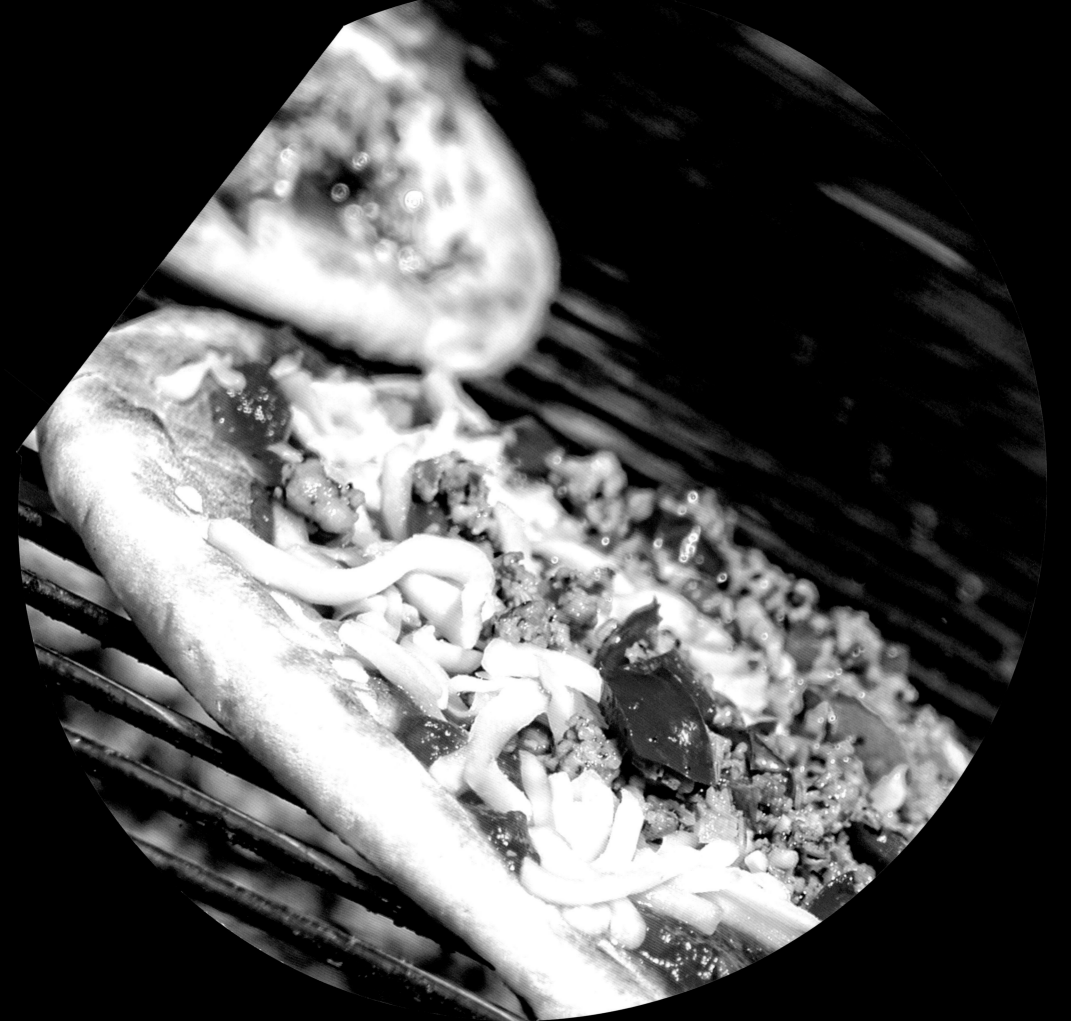

ENGLISH MUFFIN PIZZA

Original recipe makes four servings

INGREDIENTS

» 4 English muffins, split
» 2 cups shredded mozzarella cheese
» 1/2 cup canned pizza sauce
» 16 slices pepperoni sausage

DIRECTIONS

1. Preheat the oven to 375 degrees F (190 degrees C).
2. Place the English muffin halves cut side up onto a baking sheet. Spoon some of the pizza sauce onto each one.
3. Top with mozzarella cheese and pepperoni slices.
4. Bake for 10 minutes in the preheated oven, or until the cheese is melted and browned on the edges

Source: Allrecipes.com

TACO PIZZA

Original recipe makes two 12-inch pizzas

INGREDIENTS

» 10 fluid ounces warm water
» 3/4 teaspoon salt
» 3 tablespoons vegetable oil
» 4 cups all-purpose flour
» 2 teaspoons active dry yeast
» 3/4 cup water
» 1 (6 ounce) can tomato paste
» 1 (1.25 ounce) package taco seasoning mix, divided
» 1 teaspoon chili powder, or to taste
» 1/2 teaspoon cayenne pepper, or to taste
» 1 (16 ounce) can fat-free refried beans
» 1/3 cup salsa
» 1/4 cup chopped onion
» 1/2 pound ground beef
» 4 cups shredded Cheddar cheese

Directions displayed on next page

Source: Allrecipes.com

TACO PIZZA

Continued from previous page

DIRECTIONS

1. Add the water, salt, oil, flour and yeast to your bread machine in the order listed. Select the dough cycle. Check your dough after it has been mixing a few minutes. If it is too dry and not mixing, add water 1 tablespoon at a time, until the dough to be pliable but not sticky. You want the dough to be pliable but not sticky.

2. Meanwhile, in a small bowl, combine tomato paste, water, and 3/4 of the package of taco seasoning mix. Stir in chili powder and cayenne pepper; set aside. In another bowl, mix refried beans, salsa, and onion; set aside. In a large skillet, cook ground beef until evenly brown; drain excess fat. Season with the remaining 1/4 package of taco seasoning and a small amount of water. Simmer a few minutes, then remove from heat.

3. Preheat oven to 400 degrees F (200 degrees C).

4. When the dough cycle is finished, remove the dough from the machine. Divide the dough in half, and pat into two 12 inch pans. Spread a layer of the bean mixture on, then a layer of the tomato mixture. Sprinkle with seasoned beef and top with cheddar cheese.

5. Bake in preheated oven for 10 to 15 minutes, or until crust is golden brown and cheese is melted. Turn pizzas halfway through baking.

PIZZA SUPREME

Original recipe makes 4 servings

INGREDIENTS

- » 1 tablespoon olive oil
- » 1 (12 ounce) bag Birds Eye® Recipe Ready Pizza Supreme Blend
- » 1 cup prepared pizza sauce
- » 1 (10 ounce) pre-baked whole wheat or regular pizza crust
- » 1 ounce sliced pepperoni
- » 1 cup shredded mozzarella cheese

DIRECTIONS

1. Preheat oven to 450 degrees F (230 degrees C).
2. Heat oil in large nonstick skillet over medium-high heat and cook Recipe Ready Pizza Supreme Blend, stirring occasionally, 10 minutes or until vegetables are softened and any liquid is absorbed.
3. Arrange pizza crust on baking sheet and evenly spread with pizza sauce. Top with vegetable mixture and pepperoni. Sprinkle with cheese. Bake 10 minutes or until cheese is melted.

Source: Allrecipes.com

SPINACH ALFREDO PIZZA

Original recipe makes 16 servings

INGREDIENTS

» 1 (10 ounce) package frozen chopped spinach, thawed and drained
» 1 (10 ounce) container Alfredo Sauce
» 1 (6 ounce) can sliced mushrooms, drained
» 1/2 cup grated Parmesan cheese
» 1 (10 ounce) can artichoke hearts, drained and quartered
» 4 cups shredded mozzarella cheese
» 2 unbaked pizza crusts
» 2 tablespoons olive oil
» 1 (2.25 ounce) can sliced black olives (optional)

DIRECTIONS

1. Preheat the oven to 350 degrees F (175 degrees C). Spread pizza crusts out onto baking sheets or pizza pans.
2. Place the spinach and Alfredo sauce in a saucepan, and warm over medium heat. Stir occasionally. Spread 1tablespoon of olive oil onto each pizza crust. Spoon half of the Alfredo and spinach onto each crust, then arrange artichoke hearts over the sauce layer. Top each pizza with half of the mozzarella cheese and Parmesan cheese. Sprinkle mushrooms and black olives on top.
3. Bake pizzas one at a time for 20 minutes in the preheated oven, or until the bottom is nicely browned.

Source: Allrecipes.com

PIZZA MUFFINS

Original recipe makes 16 servings

INGREDIENTS

- 2 1/2 cups all-purpose flour
- 2 teaspoons baking powder
- 1/2 teaspoon baking soda
- 1/2 teaspoon salt
- 1 teaspoon dried basil leaves
- 1/2 teaspoon dried oregano
- 2 tablespoons white sugar
- 3 sun-dried tomatoes packed in oil, drained and diced
- 2 1/2 cups shredded sharp Cheddar cheese, divided
- 4 green onions, chopped
- 1 egg, beaten
- 1 1/2 cups buttermilk

DIRECTIONS

1. Preheat oven to 375 degrees F (190 degrees C). Grease muffin cups or line with paper muffin liners.

2. In a large bowl, combine flour, baking powder, baking soda, salt, basil, oregano and sugar into large bowl; stir until well blended. Mix in tomatoes, 1.5 cups of cheese and onions. In another bowl beat egg, whisk in buttermilk and stir until combined. Spoon batter into muffin tins until half full. Sprinkle remaining 1 cup cheese on top of muffins.

3. Bake in preheated oven for 15 to 20 minutes, until a toothpick inserted into center of the muffin comes out clean.

Source: Allrecipes.com

EGGPLANT PIZZA

Original recipe makes four servings

INGREDIENTS

- » 2 eggs
- » 1 cup all-purpose flour
- » 1/2 teaspoon salt
- » 1/4 teaspoon ground black pepper
- » 1/2 teaspoon dried oregano
- » 1 large eggplant, sliced into 1/2 inch rounds
- » 1/4 cup vegetable oil
- » 1 (14 ounce) can pizza sauce
- » 1 1/2 cups shredded mozzarella cheese

DIRECTIONS

1. Preheat an oven to 350 degrees F (175 degrees C).
2. Beat the eggs in a bowl. Mix the flour, salt, pepper, and oregano in a 1 gallon resealable plastic bag. Dip each eggplant slice in the egg, then drop the eggplant in the flour mixture one at a time, shaking the bag to coat the eggplant.
3. Heat the vegetable oil in a large, deep skillet over medium heat. Place the eggplant slices in the skillet to cook, turning occasionally, until evenly browned. Drain the eggplant slices on a paper towel-lined plate. Arrange the eggplant in one layer on a baking sheet. Spoon enough pizza sauce to cover each eggplant slice. Top each eggplant with mozzarella cheese.
4. Bake until the cheese is melted.

Source: Allrecipes.com

TOUCHDOWN PIZZA

Original recipe makes one 14-inch pizza

INGREDIENTS

- » 1 (14 ounce) package prebaked pizza crust (such as Boboli®)
- » 1 cup diced cooked chicken breast
- » 3 tablespoons Buffalo wing sauce
- » 1/2 cup Buffalo wing sauce
- » 1 (4 ounce) package crumbled blue cheese
- » 1 stalk celery, thinly sliced
- » 1 cup shredded mozzarella cheese

DIRECTIONS

1. Preheat oven to 475 degrees F (245 degrees C).
2. Line a baking sheet with aluminum foil. Place pizza crust on the prepared baking sheet.
3. Mix chicken and 3 tablespoons wing sauce together in a bowl until evenly coated. Spread 1/2 cup wing sauce on the pizza crust; top with mozzarella cheese, chicken mixture, and celery. Cover pizza with blue cheese.
4. Bake in the preheated oven until pizza is cooked through and cheese is bubbling, about 12 minutes. Cool pizza about 5 minutes before cutting into squares.

Source: Allrecipes.com

SHRIMP PIZZA

Original recipe makes one pizza

INGREDIENTS

- » 1 (10 ounce) container refrigerated pizza dough 1 teaspoon Italian seasoning
- » 2 tablespoons olive oil
- » 1 small red bell pepper, sliced
- » 1/2 small red onion, sliced
- » 2 teaspoons Italian seasoning
- » 2 (6.5 ounce) cans small shrimp, drainede

- » 1 (8 ounce) package cream cheese, softened
- » 1 cup grated Parmesan cheese
- » 1/2 cup mayonnaise
- » 2 cloves garlic, minced
- » 1 (10 ounce) package frozen chopped spinach, thawed and drained
- » 2 tablespoons olive oil

Directions displayed on next page

Source: Allrecipes.com

SHRIMP PIZZA

Continued from previous page

DIRECTIONS

1. Preheat an oven to 400 degrees F (200 degrees C). Stir together the cream cheese, Parmesan cheese, mayonnaise, garlic, and spinach until evenly mixed; set aside. Press the pizza dough onto a baking sheet, and brush with 2 tablespoons of olive oil. Sprinkle with 1 teaspoon Italian seasoning.

2. Bake in the preheated oven until golden brown, 10 to 12 minutes. Meanwhile, heat 2 tablespoons of olive oil in a skillet over medium heat, and cook the bell pepper and onion until tender, about 5 minutes. Season with 2 teaspoons of Italian seasoning, and stir in the canned shrimp; cook until the shrimp are heated through.

3. When the crust has baked, remove from the oven, and spread evenly with the spinach mixture. Spread the shrimp and vegetable mixture onto the pizza, and cut into pieces to serve.

4.

Source: Allrecipes.com

RUCKUS

B O O K S

Businesses looking to connect with their customers can work with Ruckus to develop their own custom 3D book. Cut through the noise of throw-away swag, and tired old tricks and sell your story, wrapped in your product. Or publish your catalog inside a lookalike shell and give it away. The impact is immediate, the shelf-life long, and the possibilities are endless. Contact us at ruckusbooks.com.

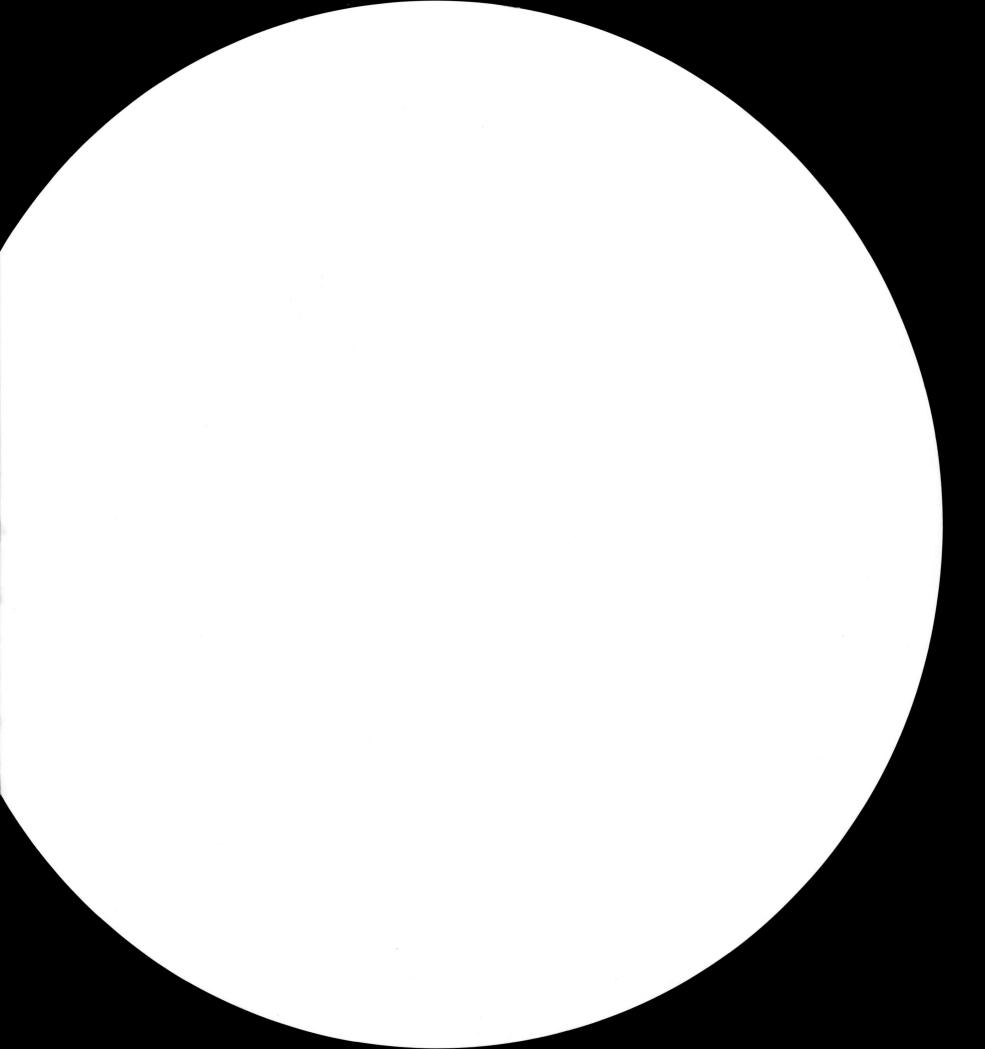